THE PRACTICAL STRATEGIES SERIES
IN AUTISM EDUCATION

series editors
FRANCES A. KARNES & KRISTEN R. STEPHENS

Families of Children With Autism: What Educational Professionals Should Know

Lee M. Marcus, Ph.D., and Ann Palmer

PRUFROCK PRESS INC.

Prufrock Press Inc.
P.O. Box 8813
Waco, Texas 76714-8813
Phone (800) 998-2208
Fax (800) 240-0333
http://www.prufrock.com

Contents

The Practical Strategies Series in Autism offers teachers, counselors, administrators, parents, and other interested parties up-to-date information on a variety of issues pertaining to the characteristics, diagnosis, treatment, and education of students with autism spectrum disorders. Each guide addresses a focused topic and is written by an individual with authority on the issue. Several guides have been published. Among the titles are:

- *An Introduction to Children With Autism*
- *Diagnosis and Treatment of Children With Autism Spectrum Disorders*
- *Educational Strategies for Children With Autism Spectrum Disorders*

For a current listing of available guides within the series, please contact Prufrock Press at 800-998-2208 or visit http://www.prufrock.com.

Acknowledgment

This book is intended for professionals who work with families of individuals with autism. The authors, one a professional and one a parent and a professional, have been involved in the field of autism for several decades and share the common perspective of the value and necessity of collaboration and partnership. TEACCH (Treatment and Education of Autistic and related Communication-handicapped CHildren), the North Carolina state-mandated agency for serving persons with autism, has been the touchstone for the beliefs and values of the authors. Under the leadership of its founder, Dr. Eric Schopler, who challenged the destructive practices of the mental health establishment in the 1960s, TEACCH pioneered many of the principles and methods of helping families that are now commonly accepted. This book is dedicated to his memory and legacy.

Although it is now widely accepted that parents of children with autism should be supported and considered part of a treatment planning team, as recently as 40 years ago parents were viewed as part of their child's problems. Parents were largely blamed for the idiosyncratic and difficult behaviors seen in their children, whose condition was considered an emotional disturbance, not the biologically based disorder that research and practice have shown today. As difficult as it was for parents to raise and cope with these challenging children, dealing with the added burden of blame and guilt was grossly unfair and harmful. Parents who were able to survive through sheer determination, courage, and single-mindedness of purpose still were scarred by their negative experiences with professionals. Others, who were unable to deal with a critical and markedly unhelpful professional community, gave up their struggle, placing their children in institutions. In some instances, parents were told early on to give their child up, partly because of the lack of available services and also because pediatricians and others failed to understand the parent perspective. Professionals today need to be aware of and appreciate what this earlier generation of parents went through and how the professionals of that era contributed to the stress of these parents.

In the middle to late 1960s, there began a shift in perspective on the causes of autism, although there was not agreement at the time that it was a biological condition. A group of psychologists demonstrated that many of the unusual behaviors of the child with autism could be changed by behavioral techniques and, eventually, treatments emphasizing emotional problems lost favor in the professional community. However, the behavioral approach was largely grounded in social learning theory that implied that the child with autism's atypical development and difficult behaviors were likely caused by environmental contingencies and faulty learning models. Parents were still considered part of the problem and cause, although the explanation was no longer rooted in psychodynamic theory, which posits that human behavior is shaped by conscious and unconscious influences.

So, on the one hand, the psychogenic approach (i.e., focusing on a psychological rather than physiological origin) considered parents from a psychotherapeutic framework, attempting to deal with the underlying emotional problems in the parents that were negatively affecting their child with autism; on the other hand, the behavioral approach provided directed instruction to parents who were expected to follow a fairly strict program to fix their child's problems. Although the latter approach was far less judgmental and more constructive, it was not intended as a cooperative partnership between parent and professional.

Several developments across a 10–15-year period from the 1960s through the 1970s influenced the direction of parent-professional relationships. In 1964, the late Bernard Rimland's (1964) book detailed his theory that autism was biologically based. Although not widely read or accepted at the time, his theory laid the groundwork for future research and the ultimate change in the understanding of the etiology and nature of autism.

In 1966, the late Eric Schopler and Bob Reichler, with funding from the National Institute of Mental Health, conducted research demonstrating that parents of children with autism could be brought into the treatment process as cotherapists (Schopler & Reichler, 1971). This revolutionary concept led to many of the current methods and practices that involve parents and professionals working in a collaborative manner. Eventually, because of the strong impact their research project had on the families it served in North Carolina, the TEACCH program was established and has become an internationally recognized and comprehensive service system, now in its fifth decade (Mesibov, Shea, & Schopler, 2005).

In 1975, the United States Congress passed the Education of all Handicapped Children Act (subsequently known as the Individuals with Disabilities Education Improvement Act or IDEA) that, among its many groundbreaking components, mandated a critical role for parents in the education planning process (IDEA, 2004). Prior to this law, the majority of school-age children with autism were either at home, in mental retardation institutions or psychiatric hospitals, and receiving little to no educational programming. Their parents had no voice or power to have any influence on obtaining appropriate services for their children. The law completely altered the situation. Children were now required to be served appropriately in the least restrictive settings and they and their parents had rights that the school systems had to provide. The blueprint for education, the Individualized Education Program (IEP), was to be based on a careful assessment of the child's needs and had to include the parents as part of the planning team. Interestingly, in the previous years, prior to the federal law, TEACCH had helped establish 10 public school classrooms, serving nearly 60 students with autism, among the first such classrooms in the country. These classroom programs embodied many of the principles of the public law, including parent involvement and individualized programming based on careful assessment.

A Developmental Framework for Understanding Families

Everything in a parent's life changes when he or she first hears the word "autism" in relationship to his or her child. Parents enter a system within the schools they never thought they would need. They find themselves working with people they never thought they would meet. Parents are suddenly driving constantly to different therapies, doctors, and special programs. When they have time they may be reading books about autism, attending conferences, or searching for more information about autism on the Internet. The parents' lives become overwhelmed with the everyday struggles of taking care of a child who may be challenging all of their parenting skills (Morrell & Palmer, 2006).

The relationships parents have also can change when their child is diagnosed. Having a child with an autism spectrum disorder (ASD) adds financial burdens to a marriage. It increases physical and emotional stress that can affect a couple's relationship. Friendships also may change when friends no longer share the same experiences. If a relationship is not very strong to begin with, it can be tested by the stresses of this experience.

When a child is diagnosed, parents may begin to think of themselves differently. They are suddenly given a challenge they could not have prepared for. Am I going to be able to do this? Am I a good enough parent to do what I need to do to help my child? And as much as parents don't want to admit, they begin to look at their child differently. They may find themselves always looking for the autism or looking for improvement or regression in their child. Parents may lose track of their child as a child and forget how to "play" with them in their efforts to "work" with them all of the time.

Helping parents survive this experience is a challenge. Because every child on the autism spectrum is unique, every parenting experience will be different. Every parent's experience will be influenced by his or her background and beliefs, family history, marital status, and financial situation. The amount of personal support parents may have will also vary. All of these factors can affect the parents' response to a diagnosis and how they work with professionals to help their child.

There is a wide range of emotions parents find themselves trying to balance when their child is diagnosed. *Fear* is a dominant emotion, especially in the beginning. Parents experience an intense fear of the future. That is why you often see a parent of a 3-year-old worrying about what that child will be like as an adult. What will the future hold for their child and what struggles will he have? Parents also are afraid for the child's safety. Will she be accepted or rejected? Will he be bullied or taken advantage of? Parents understand the vulnerability of their children and that can drive this fear.

Parents are going to feel *sad* as they deal with the loss of the child they thought they had. They also may be sad for the loss of the life they wanted for themselves and for their family. Adjusting to the diagnosis is a grieving process. Part of that grieving process involves letting go of some of the dreams a parent has for his or her child.

Parents also feel *inadequate*, especially immediately following the diagnosis. They don't know what to do or how to help their child. They have doubts about their parenting skills and the decisions they are making for their child. While dealing with the overwhelming task of finding strategies and resources to help their child, parents also are trying to learn everything they can about the diagnosis and how to advocate for the needs of their child. It is an overwhelming responsibility for the parents.

Many parents feel *guilty*. They may question whether they were responsible for this happening to their child. Parents may feel guilty about not recognizing early enough that something was wrong and waiting too long to access help. Parents also may feel guilty about not doing enough or not knowing enough about the choices they make for treatment for their child.

Parents often feel *frantic* as they are driven by the need to make up for lost time. They have to do everything possible to help their child. They have to see progress *now*. They have to try everything possible for fear of missing the one thing that could make the difference for their child.

Parents also feel *confused*. What caused this? What therapy should we use? What is normal development and what is the autism? Which professionals should we believe? Is the diagnosis correct? Parents don't have the answers and often are bombarded with conflicting information and advice.

While trying to balance all of these somewhat negative and draining emotions, parents also may feel *hopeful*. Many are hoping for a cure or hoping for a certain level of progress or achievement for their child. Sometimes the parents' hopes may seem unrealistic to the professionals helping the family. But parents need some level of hope to survive, especially during the early time following the diagnosis. It is this hopefulness that keeps parents working to help their child.

These emotions described above are especially intense following the diagnosis, but they often reappear at times throughout the parents' life with their child. They may reappear whenever the parents are facing a difficult transition for the child. They intensify whenever there is a setback in the child's progress. For many parents, the transition out of school to adult life can be a very difficult experience, much like that time following the diagnosis. Again they may be feeling overwhelmed and confused and sad. Understanding that there are triggers that intensify these emotions in parents can help a professional be more successful in supporting the family.

In addition to all of the emotions parents are dealing with, they also have to deal with the physical impact of parenting these children. Parents often are sleep deprived because many children with autism have sleep issues. They may be physically exhausted from chasing a hyperactive child. Parents of children with autism also experience continuous stress and typically have little time to relax. This ongoing stress can affect parents' physical health. Parents often will ignore their own physical and emotional needs and put their child's needs first.

Parents of children with autism deal with other *stressors*, unique to this condition, described in the following sections.

Diagnostic Confusion

Despite current widespread publicity and media attention surrounding autism, all too often parents are not given an accurate, clear, and informative description and definition of their child's challenges. Parents usually suspect early on that their child has a significant developmental problem, but often find their observations unsupported by pediatricians or other health professionals. Later when the struggles begin to escalate and a referral is made to other professionals, the diagnosis of autism may be buried in terms such as *Pervasive Developmental Disorder* or *developmental delays in social and language areas* or other equally unhelpful labels. The failure to establish or communicate the diagnosis of autism adds to the stress of coping with the difficult behaviors and learning difficulties of their child.

Uneven and Unusual Course of Development

Autism is a disorder marked by delays and deviancies in development, cutting across a variety of areas of functioning. The course of development can vary from apparently early normal development followed by plateau or regression, to generally slow development with the gradual unfolding of the autism character-istics (DeMyer, 1979). These atypical patterns are accompanied by unevenness across skill areas, such as relatively intact visual spatial and motor skills alongside deficient language, social, and problem-solving abilities. Such variability across skills and time is confusing to parents whose natural inclination is to expect normal development and deny significant problems. When their child's development seems to be slowing, parents usually will consider such a process to be temporary. When they see their child solve a complex puzzle or remember a route to a fast-food restaurant, they understandably will overlook the receptive lan-guage delays or weak imitation skills. The child's uneven profile can prove frustrating to the parents who may feel that their child will soon catch up. Gauging appropriate expectations is difficult; for example, although the child may have adequate motor skills for being toilet trained, he may not be ready if his understanding of cause and effect is limited. Parents usually communicate with their child using spoken language, along with emotional expres-sion; however, their child is not likely to respond adequately to either form of communication, heightening the parents' anxiety and confusion.

The "Can't Versus Won't" Dilemma

Related to the confusion generated by the child's uneven developmental pattern is the question of whether the child is unable to do something (e.g., respond to a request) or is simply refusing. A typical parental reaction to a child's failure to follow through is to assume that the child is unmotivated or is being stubborn. This interpretation is compounded by the child's inconsistent responses and occasional impression of understand-ing what is being asked. The child also may pick up on contex-tual cues (e.g., "time to eat" said as food is placed on the table) that suggest a greater understanding of language than is the case. When parents assume that their child is being willful and obstinate, their discipline techniques tend to be confrontational and result in negatively charged situations. Appropriate intervention can help parents recognize which behaviors are the result of lack of understanding or ability and which are oppositional. In the absence of such professional guidance, parents experience considerable stress.

Attractive Appearance

Because most children with autism appear typical, are attractive, and from the strictly physical standpoint do not stand out from their peers, parents experience additional frustration and stress when their child acts unusual or like a much younger child. Unlike obvious impairments such as blindness or cerebral palsy, autism is almost invisible, creating expectations of average social and communicative behavior that are rarely met. The discrepancy between these expectations and the reality of the disability increases the burden on the family members as they seek to understand the child's condition and how to deal with it.

Behavior in Public

A constant source of stress for parents is the potentially embarrassing behavior of their child in public places. Anxiety can be highest in parents whose child has not been diagnosed or who have not yet developed the "thick skin" necessary to cope with the myriad of predictable and unpredictable situations faced in the community. Dealing with their child having a major tantrum, disrupting a church service, approaching strangers indiscriminately, or being loud or intrusive intensifies the day-to-day stress on families. Parents understandably worry that they are being judged by others as not being able to control what appears to be a typical child by physical appearance. In addition, completing daily chores (e.g., shopping) can be a monumental task, so that family life is further disrupted.

Professional Turfism

Obtaining an accurate diagnosis can be difficult, as noted above. Adding to this stress may be disagreements among professionals, even after the proper diagnosis is made. Given the complexity of the disorder and its effect on multiple aspects of development, it is not surprising that professionals from various disciplines will advocate for treatment techniques and goals reflecting their particular perspective. Unfortunately, varying perspectives can conflict, leaving parents struggling for clarification and support. For example, a pediatric neurologist might view a seizure disorder in a child with autism as primary, treatable, and contraindicating the diagnosis of autism, even though autism and seizures often co-occur. Parents naturally will latch onto a more hopeful prognosis and develop doubts about the professionals who made the autism diagnosis. Another example might be a recommended treatment of sensory integration therapy with the goal of effecting global change in all areas of the child's functioning, not simply to help with a specific behavior (e.g., increasing the child's ability to tolerate a certain texture), a choice that seems incompatible with empirically validated educational techniques. Again, parents may be forced to choose, largely because professionals are not working collaboratively, but are committed to their methods and "turf." In these situations, the family and their child ultimately suffer.

Fads and Unproven Therapies

Like other chronic or incurable disorders, autism has been the target for quick-fix practitioners whose techniques end up victimizing families desperate for easy answers to difficult questions. The past decade seems to have spawned an extraordinary number of promised cures or solutions, far more than the previous decades. Popular interest in autism by the news media along with the advent of electronic communication, have added to the speed with which information, both accurate and distorted, is obtained. Children are being identified and diagnosed much earlier (Coonrod & Stone, 2005), and parents seek out as much information as possible, becoming susceptible to the promotions of specific therapies that usually have little to offer other than hope.

Schopler (1995) has discussed several factors these techniques have in common. For example, the technique appears to be a good idea at first impression or may have been helpful in its application to a certain condition and is now assumed to be generalizable to individuals with autism.

In addition, reports of effectiveness are invariably anecdotal and not based on careful empirical research. One or two cases of a "cure" are sufficient to capture the attention of vulnerable families. But without systematic investigation, it cannot be clear what, if any, factors specific to the treatment worked or what would happen over time with multiple cases. The written and television magazine stories are not interested in a new technique that has failed. As Schopler (1995) has noted

> replications are often based on unlikely hypotheses, without adequate theoretical bases, but promoted mainly by hype and hope. Regardless of how the techniques are repeated, not a single treatment technique has been effective with all or even most autistic children. (p. 14)

Another common factor is that these techniques invariably have negative and costly side effects. For example, the inevitable outcome of the indiscriminate use of facilitated communication has been unwarranted and unfounded accusations of sexual abuse against families whose lives have been all but destroyed. The excitement over inclusion as the single option for educating all students with autism has resulted in the failure to provide many students meaningful, individualized instruction.

Trying to sort through the claims of the various therapies so widely touted adds to parental stress. Further it diverts parents from dealing with the fundamental needs of their child and focusing energies in useful teaching and behavioral approaches.

Barriers to Building a Collaborative Relationship With Families

The diagnosis of an autism spectrum disorder suddenly propels parents into the role of advocate for their child. At a time when they are just beginning to learn about autism, it becomes the parents' job to explain, defend, and promote their children. Understandably, parents often feel unprepared and overwhelmed (Morrell & Palmer, 2006).

To be a successful advocate for their child, the first step for parents is to find professionals who can help. Parents and professionals need to work together. These children are complicated and challenging. They need all of the strategies and ideas that can be collected to help them be successful and have a good life. Working together as parents and professionals is important in combining the knowledge and experience needed to develop a comprehensive program to help the child. But creating a positive and collaborative relationship between parents and professionals takes time and effort.

Parents enter into a new relationship with a professional with their own previous history with professionals. This can be a barrier to building that collaborative relationship that is needed. The parent may have had negative experiences with professionals in the past. Their child may have been misdiagnosed. Or maybe the parents were treated as overprotective or overreactive parents, and their concerns were dismissed by a professional. The child with ASD may have been removed from a program because of behaviors or rejected because of the diagnosis. All of these kinds of experiences can make a parent mistrustful or defensive toward professionals. Parents may not feel comfortable reaching out for help if they haven't felt understood or supported in the past.

Professionals, like parents, come into a new relationship with their own history. If their previous experiences with parents were negative or difficult, they too may feel defensive. A bad experience with a parent may influence how much the professional is involved in supporting the child or communicating with the parents. Past histories can interfere with successful collaboration.

In addition to recognizing the history each party brings with it into a new parent/professional relationship, it is important to understand the stressors that each is experiencing. The emotional and physical impact of parenting these children has been discussed, but it is important to also consider the issues that educational professionals are confronting. They have to deal with the controversies about the causes and treatments for autism. There is no general agreement on what strategies work best. There also are many demands on professionals from the "system." There is documentation that needs to be done, federal and state standards that need to be met. Teachers especially spend a great deal of time completing required paperwork. And successful programs that work with students with autism must be individualized for each student. That requires juggling the needs of many and this can be very challenging and overwhelming. Understanding the challenges that both parents and professionals face is important to developing a successful working relationship.

How Professionals Can and Should
Help to Overcome the Barriers

The professional, if possible, should get to know the family. She may need to "step into their world" by learning about the family structure and family dynamics. Find out what stressors exist within the home. Are there outside supports available to the family?

It also is important to ask the parents about previous experiences with professionals. Have they had negative experiences in the past that make them hesitant to collaborate with professionals? If their previous experiences have been successful, what made them successful?

As the professional is getting to know the family, she will be learning important information about the child and how the family works with her. Professionals should respect this information and use it to prevent problems and set goals for the child. Parents have a wealth of knowledge and experience that can help the professional understand the strengths and challenges of the child. Respecting that information and using it toward helping the child will build trust between the family and the professional.

It also is very important to connect the family with any resources that can be helpful. The needs of the family often will exceed the capacity of any one professional. By connecting them to additional resources, the professional is helping the parents enlarge their circle of support. It is this circle of support within a community that will be needed throughout the life of the child.

As new parents, it is easy to focus on the child's delays and deficits. More than anyone else in the parents' lives, professionals are in the position to see their child as a child and not just the diagnosis. As we have mentioned before, parents feel very inadequate. Professionals can help parents see their strengths. Professionals may be the only ones to recognize how hard parents work and how many things they do well. Telling parents that they are doing a good job is extremely powerful in building their self-esteem and in developing parents' trust.

Never underestimate the power of listening. Conflict often is a result of poor communication. When the professional takes the time to listen to and acknowledge the point of view of the parent, she is showing her respect for the parent. She may continue to disagree but by listening well she is helping to build a collaborative trusting relationship.

Principles of Parent-Professional Collaboration

Over the years of the program, TEACCH has been in the forefront of building bridges between parents and professionals (Marcus, Kunce, & Schopler, 2005). To help parents and professionals in their efforts to effectively deal with the child's challenges, the TEACCH program has evolved a number of principles and concepts that guide treatment efforts and philosophy.

Parent-Professional Collaboration

The overriding principle of the TEACCH approach to family work involves adherence to the goal of building a collaborative relationship between parents and professionals. The belief in a partnership based on mutual respect and trust is paramount. Over the years, four types of relationships have been identified. First, parents relate to professionals as trainees, with an emphasis on home teaching programs, behavior management, and related activities. Second, parents serve as trainers of professionals with emphasis on sharing information with staff and broadening the professionals' understanding of autism and how families cope. Third, parents and professionals provide mutual emotional support, utilizing techniques of ongoing discussions, parent counseling, and support groups. Fourth, parents develop advocacy skills as a means of promoting improved services and other social action issues. Although there is no set formula applied to every case, TEACCH staff therapists and parents usually shift among these different roles in attempting to facilitate the strengthening of the parent-child relationship and to help families cope effectively with this chronic disorder.

Understanding Autism as a Developmental Disability

Perhaps the single most important concept for parents and other professionals to grasp is that autism is a disorder of development and not an emotional disturbance. Behavior problems, often the main identifying or presenting characteristic, are best viewed as the children's inability to effectively deal with their environments because of failure to adequately understand and communicate with others.

A second implication of the concept of a developmental disability is that autism is a chronic disorder that can be adapted to without being totally removed. In collaboration with parents, professionals need to be sensitive to the long-term nature of the condition and with what the parents will be faced.

A third implication is that autism is pervasive; that is, it occurs across all settings and needs to be treated accordingly. This means that a total program requires implementation in various community settings as well as the home.

Individualization and Flexibility

Although it is defined by a core set of characteristics, the wide range of manifestations of each of the major features within and across individuals reduces the likelihood that any two individuals with autism will be very similar. Persons with autism come from the entire socioeconomic spectrum and family resources vary. Therefore, in helping families, it is necessary to recognize these individual differences. A highly individualized and flexible approach requires an in-depth understanding of the child and his or her family as a point of departure during the assessment process.

Importance of Structure

A central teaching concept in the TEACCH program involves the use of structure (Schopler, Mesibov, & Hearsey, 1995). Structure is used to compensate for a child with autism's difficulties in organizing and understanding his or her world. By establishing positive routines through structured teaching, parents can capitalize on this need in their child and help develop competencies and improved learning patterns. The implication of this concept for parent training is that a clinician working with parents should use methods that effectively demonstrate the structured teaching process.

The Developmental Continuum

Not only is it important for the professional to understand autism from a developmental perspective, it is helpful to consider developmental stages in the life cycle of the family with a child with autism and the role the professional can play at different points. During early childhood, primacy is placed on early diagnosis, emotional support during the grief process, and parent training and counseling. The elementary or middle school years are ones that emphasize understanding and dealing with behavior and learning problems and home-teacher relationships. The adolescent and adult periods are a time for focusing on maximizing independence and obtaining relevant residential and work opportunities.

Competencies and Coping

The focus of intervention should be on the development and building of potential survival skills and competencies in the child and the family. The emphasis should be on pragmatic, problem-solving approaches, necessitating action-oriented approaches rather than strictly verbal interactions.

Professional as Guide, Not Expert

There is a need to respect the parental perspective and priorities and to seek out and consider parental opinion and interpretation of behavior or the proposed method of working with the child. The professional has experience with a wide range of handicapped individuals and a breadth of knowledge of what has been effective or ineffective. The parents have a deep and unique perspective on their own child's development, idiosyncrasies, likes, and dislikes. The sensitive merging of these two sources of information strengthens the parent-professional relationship toward improving the child's adaptation.

Consideration of Total Family Needs

There is a need for awareness of other pressures and demands on the family that are unrelated to the child with autism. It is easy to neglect other facets of a parent's identity and life circumstances such as economic, social, and emotional pressures. There also is a need to understand the child and family beyond the clinic or classroom; that is, the clinician should be alert to and concerned about the impact of the child on typical siblings or others in the home and the effects of the child on the parents' marital, social, and work situations. In addition, the personal or psychological implications of coping with a child with autism on a daily basis should be considered.

The fundamental approach for addressing early and ongoing needs is an education approach in which family members are helped to better understand autism, the unique needs of the child, and effective coping strategies. Substantial clinical and research evidence supports the use of parents as (co)therapists approach, both with regard to training parents in structured teaching strategies, as well as behavioral techniques and strategies. Further, families of children with autism have needs, throughout the family life cycle, for emotional, instrumental, and advocacy support. Finally, cognitive approaches have been used less frequently and explicitly, but strategies such as self-monitoring, reframing, and problem solving are used frequently when working with families of children with autism. Professionals also need to be prepared to deal with families whose problems extend beyond the stresses of having a child with autism, such as marital discord, financial hardship, or entrenched maladaptive perceptions (e.g., believing the family members have no control over life events).

A developmental perspective provides a practical framework for working with families: In early childhood, the emphasis is on early diagnosis and emotional support during the grief process, as well as parent training, counseling, and networking; in middle childhood the focus is on enhancing home-school relationships, collaboration in the design of educational programs, enhancing the development of adaptive and functional skills, and awareness of sibling issues; and the adolescent and adult periods require focus on maximizing independence and obtaining relevant vocational opportunities.

Early Childhood

Early diagnosis and assessment is the crucial first step in helping parents develop the awareness of what they face as parents of a child with autism. The manner in which they receive this information is, of course, important, although it is likely that the weight of the news of having a child with a lifelong disorder cannot be mitigated fully by any particular approach. Still, that initial conference should be structured in a way that presents the data clearly, descriptively, and sensitively without underplaying the seriousness of the situation. The age of the child, the severity of the degree of autism, and the level of intellectual and adaptive impairment to some extent control prognostic implications, but the essential nature of the condition needs to be explained.

During this session, parents need to be told that even though a precise cause may not be known, their child's disorder did not result from improper parenting or related environmental circumstances. Even if parents do not express a prior sense of guilt, there are likely to be many recriminations they attribute to themselves or live with daily. They may feel that they have not provided sufficient stimulation or should have identified the problem sooner or more aggressively sought out help. Extended family may be adding to parents' self-imposed pressure by suggesting that they are "spoiling" the child by giving in to the child's demands. The clinician who is interpreting diagnostic findings to the parents needs to be sensitive to these background factors.

Along with long-range implications of autism, parents need to understand the unique learning patterns of their child. Most likely, they have been confused by the atypical pattern of higher skills in motor development and visual memory and deficits in language and abstract problem solving. Like professionals, parents assume that the relative proficiencies suggest normal intelligence and that the child's failure to perform well in the other areas is a temporary phenomenon, a lack of motivation, or an emotional disturbance. Parents need to understand the implications of the uneven developmental profile, in particular that adequate gross motor skills should not be interpreted as potential for normal cognitive and communicative development. One of the first steps in helping parents deal effectively with their child is to establish appropriate expectations. By simplifying language demands and individualizing their teaching approach based on a realistic appraisal of developmental functioning, parents can initiate a process that will facilitate improved behavior as well as basic competencies.

Although there often are many questions raised at an interpretative conference, and detailed explanations should be provided, parents vary in their understanding and receptivity to the facts and opinions presented. The emotional impact of discovering that their child has a chronic disorder that may involve an intellectual disability as well as autism should not be underestimated. Although some families can respond with remarkable calm, it is natural to react with worry, anger, or a form of denial. In the clinic, such feelings may not be manifested, but they are likely to emerge over time. Thus, the clinician must be available for follow-up, to continue to discuss the findings and the family response, and to plan an intervention program. The clinician should be careful not to destroy the hope and optimism parents need to work with their child with autism. There is a thin line between making a "realistic prognosis" and undermining hope, and the clinician should be guided by the principle not to disturb parental expectations except when they interfere with appropriate, current management.

Along with a complete and sensitive explanation of the child's condition, the clinician should develop a systematic plan of action with the active collaboration of the family (Marcus et al., 2005). Although they may feel overwhelmed and helpless at the point of diagnosis, parents require involvement in decision making and in intervention strategies. At the outset, the momentum is provided by the professional, but parents should be given as much responsibility as they can realistically be expected to handle at this stage.

Minimally, they should be informed about, and their feelings and opinions solicited about, any treatment or additional diagnostic procedures. For example, a series of medical procedures might be recommended, including an inpatient hospital stay; but if the family is apprehensive, this plan should be postponed unless considered essential. If a preschool classroom is being considered, the parents should be encouraged to visit, ask questions of the director, and freely discuss concerns and hopes with the clinician. If a parent training, education, or a counseling program is recommended, the family's schedule and other demands and priorities that affect their time and willingness to participate should be reviewed.

During this first stage, most families are eager for maximum participation, unless other circumstances greatly prohibit this. Parents of young children with autism are themselves usually young, have more energy, and are more hopeful than parents of older children with autism. It is typical of parents to be actively involved in teaching their preschool child and in carefully scrutinizing available support services. For the parents who have just received a diagnosis, it is important to capitalize on their normal reaction to possibly reverse the course of the disorder and to gain control over the situation before the reality of the long-term implications of the condition is established. Although not every family is capable of learning specialized teaching and management skills or of becoming an articulate advocate, parents of younger children with autism tend to be well suited to carry out such tasks.

Direct parent involvement in the treatment of children with autism has become accepted as a sound and often necessary component of a total intervention program (Marcus et al., 2005). Although the models may vary in terms of methodology and content, there is no longer any dispute that the earlier psychodynamically oriented approaches have been superseded by strategies that give parents control over the teaching and therapy of their child.

As noted earlier, during these first years parents seem particularly vulnerable to quick solutions or promises of miracle cures. Some may seem far-fetched or magical, others grounded in preliminary empirical or clinical evidence. The reality is that autism is too variable and complex a condition for any one treatment to possibly address all cases. However, from the parental perspective, the popular literature and news media fail to critically evaluate claims for treatment success, and parents appropriately seek out advice from professionals as they pursue the best available services for their child. Professionals have a responsibility to keep abreast of such developments and, while keeping a critical but open mind, to be ready to handle parental questions in an as frank, but not overly judgmental, way as possible. Above all, the parents' wish to find an answer or partial solution needs to be acknowledged without encouraging them to actively pursue every lead or unsubstantiated promise of a cure.

Elementary School Years

For many families, the elementary school years are relatively less stressful than the preschool years, particularly if an adequate school program is available. As the child develops cognitively and socially, behavioral difficulties often diminish in intensity and frequency. If parents have had early identification and support, they have learned basic management and coping skills, and the child is prepared for adjusting to the public school environment. Of course, if early services have not at all been provided then families continue in a state of limbo and pressures mount. Fortunately, in the past decade improved early diagnosis and intervention services have reduced the likelihood of complete absence of services for most families with a child with autism.

The transition to the public school system is not necessarily a uniformly positive experience. Although parents are satisfied that their child is a part of a community system, they are again reminded of the chronicity and severity of their child's disability, because for many children with autism, education means placement in a special class or a special school. In addition to the usual normal anxieties parents face when their child goes to school for the first time, parents of a child with autism also have to deal with the recognition that theirs is an atypical child who is not truly integrated in the mainstream. Parents whose child is fully included in a typical classroom setting also have a number of experiences that emphasize their child's atypical development. For many parents, these events reawaken the anguish associated with the first awareness of having a child with autism and provide further evidence that the future course of development will not be normal.

The public school system is more impersonal than the typical preschool environment, and parents are far less likely to have the built-in support network they have previously experienced. Many parents who have had their child served in a developmental day care program or public school preschool program with additional family support services have appreciated the informal, caring atmosphere of a small program, often staffed with a social worker or parent coordinator. Because the main business of public schools is education, ancillary personnel are in shorter supply and are spread thinly across large numbers of children.

Parents need to be prepared for this change, and the helping clinician again should be available for advice and guidance. As in the selection of a preschool program, the clinician should be knowledgeable about the variety of early elementary programs that are appropriate and should explore these possibilities with the parents, school system personnel, and preschool teacher or other representatives. Again, parents should be central to the decision-making process, although reality usually results in relatively few options, many of which may be unacceptable or at least far from ideal. The active intervention of the professional at this stage in transition can ease the concerns of parents justifiably worried about their child's adaptation to public school, establish a foundation for a satisfactory relationship between home and the school, and indicate to the school system that the family and child have an outside advocate and support they can draw upon when school begins.

If such groundwork is successfully laid, the clinician can facilitate the development of a smooth relationship between the family and teacher. Sometimes the child's elementary school classroom does not change, and if a teacher remains with a program, the child may have the same teacher for as many as 5 to 7 years. Although this arrangement may have the advantages of continuity and consistency, from the standpoint of parent-teacher relationships there will be a natural tendency for conflicts to occur and possible competitive feelings to arise. The clinician should be alert to such tensions and may at times serve as a mediator or troubleshooter, to make certain that the teacher and the family understand each other's perspective. If the child and family are no longer seen regularly by the professional, it may be useful to conduct an annual evaluation involving the teacher to provide an objective forum to review everyone's concerns. For the teacher, questions concerning medications or development of possible seizures may arise, and the clinician should help explore this in conjunction with the parents.

Many school systems advocate full inclusion (Kauffman & Hallahan, 1995; Kluth, 2003) of all special education students, including those with autism. Although inclusion seems to be defined in various ways, its strict interpretation is full-time placement in regular education with whatever supports are necessary. Parents whose children are fully included may have mixed feelings about this arrangement: on the one hand, excited and hopeful about the opportunity of their child being educated alongside typically developing peers; on the other hand, worried about whether their child will get the individualized attention he or she needs and how successful the integrated experience will be. The professional engaged with the family whose child is included needs to be alert to the parents' emotions about the situation as well as be available to help the school program handle the variety of problems that will inevitably occur.

In addition to promoting a strong home–school relationship, the clinician should be available to continue to help the family with the child's home functioning. As the responsibility for education shifts from home to school, the focus of intervention correspondingly shifts from home teaching of the child to activities and methods that facilitate the child's continued survival and growth in the family system. Some parents may wish to remain active in basic skills training, in order to supplement the school program or as a means for feeling an integral part of the child's development. Parents have recognized that structured teaching and home routines enhance their personal interactions with their child who typically does not respond to normal conversation interchanges or family leisure events.

For most families, this stage is an auspicious time to build daily living and functional communication skills as they come to realize the importance of these areas for their child's future adaptation. Many parents, after being frustrated in their efforts to teach complex cognitive skills, are gratified at the relative ease with which their child with autism learns household routines and tasks. The individual with autism's predilection toward orderliness can be recognized by the family as a pleasant quality that fits in with everyday chores. The clinician can help by encouraging parents to work on these skills and by suggesting task analysis and other teaching techniques.

Adolescence

Over the past decade, there has been a dramatic increase in the awareness of autism in adolescence and a proliferation of writing on this topic (Howlin, Goode, Hutton, & Rutter, 2004). This surge of interest has been stimulated, in large part, by the openly expressed needs of parents whose younger children with autism were now growing older and continuing to show the major characteristics of autism. Basically, this was the same group of parents who previously helped build public awareness and program support for younger children with autism. Now faced with issues of managing and dealing with their adolescent and adult children with autism, these parents approached the professional community for methods and services to help with the next stages in their child's development.

The problems and concerns raised by families during the adolescent period reflect the continuation of earlier issues such as the chronicity of the basic deficits, the need for specialized services, dealing with the community, and the realization that the disorder is lifelong. Added to these are newer factors brought by the physical changes in adolescence, increasing sexuality and inappropriate ways of expressing it, the stress of many years of raising a child with autism, the emerging sense of independence in someone who lacks many of the prerequisites for self-direction, onset of seizures for some adolescents, and an increased awareness of the parents' own mortality. Research has indicated that this period produces additional stress for families of individuals with autism. The need for ongoing parental support is perhaps even greater as the parents' energy level decreases and their potential for burnout increases.

Behavioral matters that are likely to emerge include increased sexual awareness, aggressiveness and openly expressed defiance, and striving for independence despite limitations imposed by the disorder. These issues, of course, are common in adolescence, but the individual hampered by dysfunctions in communication, social understanding, and cognitive facility cannot cope as readily with the profound biological changes this stage brings.

The direct help that can be provided by the clinician at this point includes discussion with parents of the implications of adolescence for a person with autism; suggestions on behavior management geared to the practical realities of the home situation; sex management and counseling; relaxation and/or cognitive behavioral therapy; consideration of medication, which often becomes more necessary during this period; information regarding respite care, including afterschool, weekend, and summer options; and work toward obtaining a future residential placement. The latter consideration often comes as a jolt to families that, during the preadolescent years, rarely thought that their child could not remain at home indefinitely. The combination of their own decreasing control of the situation, other family needs and priorities, and the visible daily reminder that their child is becoming a young adult has an unexpected impact that few families have anticipated.

For many families, there is a need to develop a plan of action regarding residential placement that takes into account both logistical and emotional considerations. From the practical standpoint, an appropriate group home or other residential options may not be available, and parents need to work with community agencies to develop such a program. The clinician has to collaborate with the parent in this effort. Emotionally, parents need to know that placement outside the home is a natural and logical next step in the move toward independence of the child and not the result of the family's failure to provide a good home. Unfortunately, emergencies often allow little opportunity for adequate preparation, and placement occurs in a somewhat traumatic manner. The clinician needs to be sensitive to the emotional pain experienced by parents in these circumstances and should thoughtfully counsel them through the crisis. As with parents of younger children, support groups for the parents of adolescents remain crucial as they continue to seek solutions to daily problems and quality services.

The other area for parental support involves the changing educational needs of the adolescent with autism. Parents who have worked tirelessly to obtain adequate early school programs often have to follow the same route to continue their child's education into secondary schools. If the school system has not planned ahead, the adolescent with autism may be left adrift or kept in the elementary school setting despite the chronological age discrepancy. In addition, with increased age, the type of curriculum must shift in most cases away from academic to prevocational and vocational. Parents should be prepared for this as early as possible and should be supported by the clinician outside the educational system in their efforts to obtain a suitable educational setting and curriculum.

Finally, in the absence of full-time residential care, the professional should help locate adequate respite and emergency relief services, afterschool and recreational programs, and summer programs. These services are required to some extent at all stages of development, but they become particularly critical as the child grows older.

From the standpoint of the role of the professional over time, although the need to remain engaged in a partnership remains constant, the scope of activities broadens, with less emphasis on direct treatment of the child and greater initiative in interacting with the community and alertness to crisis situations.

Adulthood

Although the primary focus of this book is on the school-age years, it remains important to address issues of adulthood. Relatively little has been written about autism in adulthood, compared to early childhood, beyond outcome studies (Howlin et al., 2004), parental narratives (e.g., Park, 1982), and aspects of treatment and care (Howlin, 2004). More recently, autobiographies of high-functioning persons with autism have become popular and highlighted coping and adjustment problems in this subgroup (e.g., Tammet, 2006). What is known is that the problems of autism continue to some extent, that impairment in cognitive and social adaptation persists, and that the needs for long-range sheltered care and supervised employment pertain to the majority. The assistance that families require is consistent with that required during the adolescent period, but the ability of most families to continue to take the initiative in procuring services is considerably compromised by their declining strength.

Historically, by adulthood most individuals with autism have been institutionalized; however, the recent efforts at deinstitutionalization is likely to all but eliminate that option, and the responsibility of the home and community to arrange for residential care and vocational opportunities has become more prevalent. Thus, there is a greater urgency for the professional to explore these options with families and, more so than ever before, to take a leadership role in creating opportunities and advocating in the community. Certainly by their early adulthood years persons with autism should have the opportunity to live independently, whether in a group home, apartment complex with supervision, or comparable facility. Parents of adults with autism should be able to have the same expectations as parents of typical individuals to see their adult offspring live his or her life away from home.

With school services no longer available, job training and placement become a top priority, and although some families have options available, in most situations the adult with autism will be at home, increasing the burden on parents. The professional must anticipate this situation before the conclusion of the school years and work toward an appropriate day program, and, it is hoped, meaningful employment.

Parents also need to be involved in estate planning, guardianship, and related matters that affect the future of their adult with autism. Again, the professional can be available to remind the parent of this and should also be aware of legal counsel experienced in this area.

Direct services that can be helpful include individual counseling with higher functioning adults, social skills training and related social activities, and parent support groups. If the adult with autism has received adequate educational services and parents have been actively involved in their child's programs and received good support for themselves, then the shift into adulthood can be smooth and rewarding. The parent-professional partnership can continue to be productive.

Additional Tips for Professionals Working With Families

Whether the professional is a teacher, psychologist, psychiatrist, speech therapist, occupational therapist, social worker, or other, the following tips can be helpful and should be carefully considered. Some are general suggestions, while others are specific.

Realize That Parents Are Grateful

Although there are times that parents seem to be demanding and focused exclusively on their child and may appear unappreciative, they really are grateful for the help and support of professionals. In the middle of an IEP discussion or struggling with a difficult behavior problem, parents will not be able to stop and thank the professional for listening or caring about their child, but they do appreciate that others are involved and they are not alone.

Parents Have an Emotional Bond That Needs to Be Understood

Historically, parents often have been accused of being overly involved, perhaps overprotective, and emotionally blinded. To some extent, these descriptors are accurate, but should not be used by professionals to judge parents or to dismiss their perspective. Rather, professionals simply need to understand and appreciate the deep connection parents experience with their child, try to empathize, and not allow the strong feelings to disrupt the working relationship.

Anger as a Smokescreen

Related to the previous point, parents sometimes will express anger to professionals, which can create a barrier to effective communication and problem solving. The anger might be directed to the teacher or at the school system. However, the anger often conceals a more basic fear or deep-seated worry about their child's future or their own struggles to help their child. Professionals should avoid getting caught up in the angry feelings being expressed, recognizing that there are other issues at play.

Importance of Ongoing Communication

Teachers and others who have daily interaction with the child need to be in constant communication with parents, even though this can be time-consuming. Parents deeply value any notes, in whatever format they take. Their child typically cannot report on what has happened at school or other settings, so parents are totally dependent on others for information. The notes should be positive, even if negative behaviors have occurred. The brief report can list highlights of the day as well as questions for the parents to address. Do not underestimate the powerful effect a positive comment can have for the family, because much of what parents hear involves criticisms and shortcomings.

Partner, Do Not Compete With the Parents

The cornerstone of the TEACCH program, as noted earlier, is the commitment to working with parents as partners. There is an understandable tendency at times for teachers and others strongly involved with their students with autism to believe that they know what is "best" for the child based on successes in the classroom. Such a conviction can lead to an undesirable competition with the parent. Even if the strategies are working and the teacher has developed useful ideas, the child continues to be the responsibility of the parent. The teacher and other professionals have a transient relationship with the child and can be most helpful to the parents by sharing and collaborating.

Be a Good Listener

There are times that simply listening to the parents is sufficient to be supportive. Not every situation or problem requires an immediate solution. Allowing the parent to talk things through and "vent," if needed, often can lead to a resolution.

See the Child as a Person, not Just a Label

It is important to remember that autism describes only part of a child, that much more than the diagnosis shapes and determines his or her personality and character. Although autism plays a significant role in affecting learning and behavior, varying greatly across individuals, seeing the child as a total person, and conveying that to the parents, is essential to being an effective professional.

For Administrators

Administrators should become as knowledgeable as possible about autism as an educational disability and understand the parent perspective, so that while supporting teachers and support staff, they can maintain that perspective and intervene as objectively as possible during the inevitable home–school conflicts that arise.

Conclusion

This book, written from an integrated perspective of an experienced professional and a parent/professional, has touched upon a wide range of issues relevant for building and sustaining productive relationships between the helping community and families. Ultimately, what is at stake is what is in the best interests of the child and it should be self-evident that sharing that belief needs to be the focal point of all interactions. But, the path to such a shared value has many obstacles and challenges. The authors have attempted to identify the trouble spots as well as the attitudes and strategies needed to overcome the problems. In the end, both professionals and families can benefit and grow stronger from their partnerships.

Autism Society of North Carolina
http://www.autismsociety-nc.org
Provides information about the services of the society, blogs, and access to the largest bookstore in the world for materials on autism.

Beach Center on Disability
http://www.beachcenter.org
Provides parent training, professional and emotional support, education, and training materials to assist families who have members with disabilities and to influence national policy regarding the welfare of all persons with developmental disabilities. The website includes a quarterly newsletter.

Family Village
http://www.familyvillage.wisc.edu
Represents a global community of disability-related resources that integrates information, resources, and communication opportunities on the Internet for persons with cognitive and

other disabilities, their families, and those that provide them services and supports.

TEACCH (Treatment and Education of Autistic and related Communication-handicapped CHildren)
http://www.teacch.com
Provides information about the North Carolina state-mandated agency serving persons with autism and their families and includes a diverse range of articles, description of TEACCH programs, lists of ongoing training opportunities, and useful links.

Wrightslaw
http://www.wrightslaw.com
Up-to-date information about effective advocacy for children with disabilities. There are hundreds of articles, cases, newsletters, and other information about special education law and advocacy in the Wrightslaw libraries.

Coonrod, E. E., & Stone, W. L. (2005). Screening for autism in young children. In F. R. Volkmar, R. Paul, A. Klin, & D. Cohen (Eds.), *Handbook of autism and pervasive developmental disorders* (3rd ed., pp. 707–729). Hoboken, NJ: Wiley.

DeMyer, M. K. (1979). *Parents and children in autism.* New York, NY: Wiley.

Howlin, P. (2004). *Autism and Asperger syndrome: Preparing for adulthood.* London, England: Taylor Routledge.

Howlin, P., Goode, S., Hutton, J., & Rutter, M. (2004). Adult outcome for children with autism. *Journal of Child Psychology and Psychiatry, 45*, 212–229.

Individuals with Disabilities Education Improvement Act, Pub. Law 108-446 (December 3, 2004).

Kauffman, J. M., & Hallahan, D. P. (1995). *The illusion of full inclusion.* Austin, TX: Pro-Ed.

Kluth, P. (2003). *"You're going to love this kid!" Teaching students with autism in the inclusive classroom.* Baltimore, MD: Brookes.

Marcus, L. M., Kunce, L. J., & Schopler, E. (2005). Working with families. In F. R. Volkmar, R. Paul, A. Klin, & D.

Cohen (Eds.), *Handbook of autism and pervasive developmental disorders* (3rd ed., pp. 1055–1086). New York, NY: Wiley.

Mesibov, G. B., Shea, V., & Schopler, E. (2005). *The TEACCH approach to autism spectrum disorders*. New York, NY: Kluwer Academic/Plenum.

Morrell, M. P., & Palmer, A. (2006). *Parenting across the autism spectrum: Unexpected lessons we have learned*. London, England: Jessica Kingsley.

Park, C. C. (1982). *The siege*. Boston, MA: Little, Brown.

Rimland, B. (1964). *Infantile autism: The syndrome and its implications for a neural theory of behavior*. Upper Saddle River, NJ: Prentice-Hall.

Schopler, E. (1995). *Parent survival manual: A guide to crisis resolution in autism and related developmental disorders*. New York, NY: Plenum.

Schopler, E., Mesibov, G. B., & Hearsey, K. (1995). Structured teaching in the TEACCH system. In E. Schopler & G. B. Mesibov (Eds.), *Learning and cognition in autism* (pp. 243–268). New York, NY: Plenum.

Schopler, E., & Reichler, R. J. (1971). Parents-as-cotherapists in the treatment of autistic children. In S. Chess & A. Thomas (Eds.), *Annual progress in child psychiatry and child development* (pp. 679–697). New York, NY: Brunner/Mazel.

Tammet, D. (2006). *Born on a blue day: Inside the extraordinary mind of an autistic savant*. New York, NY: Simon & Schuster.

Lee M. Marcus, Ph.D., is a consulting psychologist with TEACCH and the former Clinical Director of the Chapel Hill TEACCH Center where he oversaw diagnostic, treatment, and consultation services for children, adolescents, and adults with autism. Treatment and Education of Autistic and related Communication-handicapped CHildren provides services throughout North Carolina to autistic individuals and families enabling meaningful and independent functioning within the community. He also is a clinical professor in the Department of Psychiatry at the University of North Carolina School of Medicine, where he served as director of the clinical psychology internship program from 1984–2008. Dr. Marcus received the Professional of the Year Award, presented by the Autism Society of North Carolina, in 1994. He has served on the editorial board for the *Journal of Autism and Developmental Disorders* since 1999 and was the 2000, 2006, and 2008 recipient of the Judy T. Konanc Award for outstanding supervision in psychology internship training. In 2005, he received the Joseph E. Bryan Public Service Award from the Carolina Center for Public Service. He was given the Serena Merck Leadership Memorial Award in 2006 by the National Association for the Dually Diagnosed and the Mary Clarke Award presented by the North Carolina Psychological Association in 2007. Nationally and internationally, he leads seminars, workshops, and training sessions for professionals on various topics in autism. Dr. Marcus has written extensively on issues in assessment, program development, and working with families.

Ann Palmer is the parent of a 27-year-old son with autism and is the Director of Advocacy and Chapter Support for the Autism Society of North Carolina. She coordinates more than 45 chapters and support groups across the state. Previously, she was the Parent Support Coordinator for Division TEACCH. There, she developed a volunteer parent mentor program that served five TEACCH centers and provided support to more than 800 families in North Carolina. Ann has published two books: *Realizing the College Dream With Autism or Asperger Syndrome: A Parent's Guide to Student Success*, and *Parenting Across the Autism Spectrum: Unexpected Lessons We've Learned*, the Autism Society of America's 2007 Literary Work of the Year, which she coauthored with Maureen Morrell. Both books are published by Jessica Kingsley Publishers. She also has been published in the *Journal of Autism and Developmental Disorders*; the *MAAP*, the newsletter of the MAAP Services for Autism and Asperger Syndrome; *Exceptional Parent* magazine; and *Tweens and Teens News Magazine*.